GUILT
How to Deal with It

John Hamrogue, C.SS.R.
and
Joseph Krastel, C.SS.R.

LIGUORI
PUBLICATIONS

One Liguori Drive
Liguori, Missouri 63057
(314) 464-2500

Imprimi Potest:
John F. Dowd, C.SS.R.
Provincial, St. Louis Province
Redemptorist Fathers

Imprimatur:
+ Edward J. O'Donnell
Vicar General, Archdiocese of St. Louis

ISBN 0-89243-256-X
Library of Congress Catalog Card Number: 86-82783
Cover design by Pam Hummelsheim

Copyright © 1986, Liguori Publications
Printed in U.S.A.

All rights reserved. No part of this book may be reproduced, stored in a retrieval system, or transmitted without the written permission of Liguori Publications.

Scripture texts used in this work are taken from the NEW AMERICAN BIBLE, copyright © 1970, by the Confraternity of Christian Doctrine, Washington, D.C., and are used by permission of copyright owner. All rights reserved.

Introduction

Why do people have guilt feelings about their sense of guilt? Perhaps the answer to that question lies in the differing definitions of the word *guilt*. *The American Heritage Dictionary of the English Language* gives these two meanings among others: First: "The fact of being responsible for an offense or wrongdoing." Second: "Remorseful awareness of having done something wrong." So the same word can mean a *fact* or indicate a *feeling*. We still tell our children about little George Washington, who told his father, "I cannot tell a lie. I chopped down your cherry tree. I did it with my little hatchet." He really had done it, and having done it he saw it was right to own up to it. Good for George. And good for our children to model themselves after him. But suppose little George had not chopped down the tree. Someone had, of course, and the father had gotten so angry that it made George nervous enough to feel like he had something to do with it. Though he had not done it, he made the same confession — in all sincerity. That story we would never tell our children.

Things like that do happen to children and to grown-ups. How many children, for instance, feel somehow to blame for the arguments between their parents, or for the divorce of their parents? And how often do we grown-ups feel guilt without real cause; how often are we made to feel guilty when, in fact, we are not actually responsible for any wrong?

Fact and feeling tend to become confused. We use the same word to indicate differing concepts. We come to think that fact must underlie feeling, that where there is smoke there is fire. But this is not always so, as we will see by the questions included in this booklet.

GUILT
How to Deal with It

What do modern experts say about guilt?

Sigmund Freud once wrote, "The sense of guilt is the most important problem in the development of civilization." Among other things, he meant that civilization has used guilt as a tool to enable people to live together. Where littering is looked down upon, for instance, streets will be clean because people will be ashamed of trash on them. In individual human beings he traces the earliest experiences of guilt to matters like toilet training. With a little effort we can imagine the eyes and feelings of a child as he tries to do the right thing by his parents, who are giants in his eyes and the source of all approval and satisfaction. Freud saw guilt as an important fact of life, though he opposed unrealistic or neurotic guilt.

For most practitioners in the mental health professions, guilt is a form of anxiety. There are two kinds of guilt: *realistic* guilt, corresponding to some failure or injury done to another and proportionate to the fault, and *neurotic* guilt, based on fantasy: the person feels guilty for something he or she did not do, or the experience of guilt goes beyond the culpability of the person. In many cases, psychologists leave realistic guilt to the legal profession; they spend hours and make a lot of money trying to relieve people of neurotic guilt. Because of their emphasis on neurotic guilt, some members of the mental health profession give the impression that people should not feel *any* guilt. But this attitude can lead to a minimization of realistic guilt and practically destroy any sense of responsibility for one's decisions and actions.

Many professionals in the fields of sociology, criminal justice, and race relations question *individual* guilt. These "determinists" maintain that people are compelled by their family background, lack of education, bad environment, etc., to act in a given way and that they should not be called "guilty" of robbery, drug use, etc., because they really are not free; they have been programmed toward a life of crime because of their background. Although there is a grain of truth in the observations of these professionals, they go too far in absolving people of any personal responsibility for their acts. We are all weak and influenced by others, but the number of people who have overcome poor family situations or slum backgrounds to become men and women of integrity shows that we are free and ultimately should feel guilty if we trample on the rights of others or disregard the good of the community.

In the years after the Second World War, "existentialist" novelists, philosophers, and playwrights influenced the thinking of countless people. Men like Jean Paul Sartre, Albert Camus, and others considered guilt a cruel joke. Obsessed with the absurdity of human life, they saw people suffering for nothing and working terribly hard with nothing to show for it. They did not believe in a God who cared about what happened or who directed a world he created. These men believed luck and fate determined the outcome of human hopes and struggles. The cynicism of the existentialists saw that people with a sense of responsibility and a realistic sense of guilt were often deluded and turned out to be victims of fate and the absurdity of human existence. Basically, the existentialists deny human freedom in the sense that we Christians believe in it.

Overall, many modern writers often mislead people about guilt. In some ways, Freudians and some social theoreticians are most interested in studying the phenomenon of modern guilt. They are fascinated at the mental suffering that guilt brings to so many people. But in wanting to give absolution and to free people from the burden of guilt, these writers sometimes go too far. They weaken our awareness of human freedom and brush aside our responsibility for our actions. Therefore, instead of helping us to understand and cope with realistic guilt, they often hinder us from obtaining an accurate picture of this anxiety and regret.

What does the Church say about guilt?

She takes up the teaching of the Scriptures and insists that each individual enjoys a basic personal freedom to choose between good and evil, and bears responsibility for that choice and its consequences. In Ezekiel (18:2), the prophet unforgettably argues these points when he speaks (as prophets do) with the Lord God. The two are discussing this saying of the time:

"Fathers have eaten green grapes,
 thus their children's teeth are on edge."

This proverb would have people believe that their lives are determined by the evil of their family background. Since the family was a wide grouping of people, this old saying comes pretty close to the modern determinist ideas we mentioned in the previous question.

Well, God tells Ezekiel that he will have none of this viewpoint. He insists that the father and the son, each in his own life and self, will be saved or lost in accord with the kind of life he leads. He will be saved if he keeps the moral law; he will be lost if he does not keep it. God goes on to say that the virtuous man must watch out, lest he give himself to evil and thus be lost. And in like manner he says the evil man who turns to God and goodness will be saved. For people are not born forever good or bad so that they need not worry about their choices in life. God insists that he does not wish the death and loss of anyone, but he will not back off from these conditions of life and death, even though the people accuse him of unfairness. Turning their argument against them, God accuses them of unfairness because they seek to evade the responsibility of their personal freedom and conversion to their Lord. He does not allow them to blame their guilt on their background.

Jesus, of course, takes up this teaching of the Old Testament and clearly makes it his own. We need only look to his famous parable on the final judgment in Matthew 25:31-46. There each one is saved or lost according to his or her treatment of the poor, the naked, the hungry, the outcast. In a telling line the lost exclaim (as the saved did, too) that they did not know it was Jesus in these people. Their ignorance would surely excuse them. It does not!

We can also look at John 4:4-42, which details the story of the Samaritan woman. When Jesus comes close to her sin and shame, she tries to avoid the issue by arguing religion with him. But by the time the story ends, he has told her everything she has done and she has accepted the fact of his judgment, taken responsibility for her life, and found peace and joy in his forgiveness.

In the sacrament of Penance, the Catholic Church most pointedly insists that we personally and individually take responsibility for our lives and our wrongdoings. This sacrament is Jesus' individual meeting with each of us. He met the rich Zacchaeus up in a tree, the Samaritan woman at a well, and he meets the likes of us in a reconciliation room.

The Church has long known, of course, that some people are not competent, not responsible, and that all people are sometimes excused by reason of fear, confusion, or blameless ignorance. Like anyone else, she knows that background and environment powerfully influence our choices for good and evil. But in God's name she guards the reality of human dignity and freedom, the human spirit that God breathed into the clay of the first human being. Because Jesus preached it, she also preaches the grim doctrine of hell, since it underscores how seriously God takes the power of our freedom. Astonishingly, we really can so fly in the face of his will and his laws of goodness as to fling ourselves into the eternal opposite of all good and beauty, the black hole we call hell. May we never see it. But how awesome to know we have the *freedom* and the *responsibility* to choose!

Then I suppose I have to make up my own mind about good and evil, right?

Right. We all have to make up our own minds about good and evil in our lives. This means that we must develop our consciences. It does not mean, however, that we decide on our own what is good and what is evil. God has decided what is right and what is wrong. Remember what happened to our first parents. They decided to choose for themselves when Satan told them that the forbidden fruit would not work harm on them. In fact, eating it would make them like God himself! In other words, they would be able to make their own rules about what was right and wrong. This is the supreme temptation: to covet God's right to make rules for us. We foolishly believe we can make evil work for us. Cheating can get us into a school, lying can get us a job, adultery can bring us seeming comfort. But what a price we pay!

We must seek a right or correct conscience. On this level it makes no sense to say, "My conscience says it's all right," even when that conscience flies in the face of the teachings of the Church or even of the Commandments. Conscience is a limited and delicate instrument, basically a warning system. It is something like a smoke alarm, which can save our lives but more often it annoys us by squealing over burnt toast or charred roast. Warning systems set us to checking out the real case, whether there is a fire or just smoke. In the field of morality, the law of God and the teaching of the Church in Christ's name are the standards by which we form our consciences.

At times this law of God is more than we can bear. It accuses us. This is why we sometimes make the mistake of insisting that our conscience approve of what we are doing. For we do not like to admit to sin; and even more frightening, we may fear that the law is beyond us. It may be — for now. Our late Holy Father, Paul VI, is well-known for his encyclical letter which insisted on the Church's traditional stance on contraception. He is not so well-known for his wisdom and compassion in cases of conscience. He recognized that even good people, at some times in their lives, may find some important parts of the moral law beyond their keeping. He insisted that this should not so discourage them that they avoid the Church and her sacraments. In this gentleness he was following Jesus Christ, who insisted that he came not for virtuous people but for sinners (see Matthew 9:13).

The Catholic Church is a Church of sinners because it is the Church of Jesus Christ. During his life he could meet sinful people where they were, even if they were up a tree like Zacchaeus (Luke 19:5). The Catholic Church, too, can wait for sinful people to find the heart to clamber down from their trees of unawareness. Until that time she cannot and they must not pretend that what is wrong is somehow all right, that the law of God does not bind.

Meanwhile, the best thing for us to do is to approach the sacrament of Penance in a spirit of openness to God's saving grace. There is no reason for our sins to chase us from our Mother, the Church.

Wait a minute! Aren't religion and the Church the causes of guilt to begin with?

Some people claim that severely religious parents, hard moral obligations, and preaching of divine punishment tossed them into long bouts with worry and shame. They bitterly believe that if religion had not been part of their lives they would be able to manage their guilt. Maybe the religion they got was bad religion, which will make a hard life only harder. A simple rule has it that good religion teaches us to *love* God and bad religion teaches us to *fear* him.

In some ways this problem is like the chicken-and-the-egg

question: which came first, guilt or religion? In strict history probably no one knows for sure, but quite probably religion — the more or less organized type — came on the scene to help people deal with guilt. The stain or the blot of an image of guilt comes down to us from the very ancient past, beyond any record we have of religion. In the human race and in every human being, guilt goes way back.

Religion calls people's attention to sin and the possibility of eternal loss of God because both are real. Christ, who came to free people from the threat of everlasting death, still stressed the awesome implications of human freedom: By sinning we can choose to separate ourselves from God for all eternity.

Ironically, true and good religion will sharpen the sense of guilt by stressing the commandments, by forming more sensitive consciences, and by reminding us of the gap between religious and moral ideals and the way we live. But its purpose is not to torture us; rather, its intent is to give us the courage and the means to recognize our moral wounds and seek aid for them. Christ has stressed that all of us have sinned and lost the right to heaven. But his Scriptures also focus our attention on his death for our sins, his loving invitation to eternal life, and his constant willingness to forgive us, no matter how badly we have sinned. Though Christ's religion preaches the reality of sin and judgment, it also preaches the reality of his love and mercy.

Sadly, some people think that they can escape their feelings of guilt by rejecting their religious backgrounds. They never really succeed in doing this. They often find that their consciences still irritate them when they offend others or break laws. Sometimes guilt stalks them in new and hidden ways — with moods of depression, psychosomatic illnesses, etc., which they find harder to grapple with than religious guilt. When they finally wake up, they realize that the only way to get rid of guilt is to apologize and receive forgiveness. Gradually they come back — like the prodigal son — to their Father's home. There they find a realistic approach to right and wrong and the wonderful mercy of a loving God.

But does the Church also teach about the existence of a corporate guilt that lies upon the whole human race?

Certainly. Her teaching on original sin has a most critical place in our understanding of guilt and sin. Here again the Scriptures provide a starting point. In his Letter to the Romans (see especially 5:12-19), Saint Paul teaches that Adam's sin infected the entire human race. "But how can that be?" you ask. He does not try to explain it, probably figuring we would all know it is a mystery anyway, but one of which we have some sense and feeling. John Donne's lines, "No man is an island," make sense to us. And when he writes futher, "Ask not for whom the bell tolls, it tolls for thee," we understand that, too. Other people's tears draw out our own, and we find their laughter infectious. We identify with athletes and actors, take on the shame of the failure and disgrace of "one of our own." (The people of Germany are terribly weighed down by the atrocities of the Nazis, though most of them had not yet been born at the time.) There is a *solidarity* among all human beings, and it is to this fact of life that Saint Paul refers.

The doctrine of original sin would be distorted and Saint Paul ill-served if we stopped at the point of sin and guilt. Only in speaking of Jesus Christ does Saint Paul bring the teaching on original sin to its pivotal point. His great concern is salvation, not sin. Unfortunately, religion sometimes gets so entangled with concern for sin that it tortures people's consciences. At any rate, Saint Paul was leading up to this: "Just as a single offense brought condemnation to all men, a single righteous act brought all men acquittal and life. Just as through one man's disobedience all became sinners, so through one man's obedience all shall become just" (Romans 5:18-19). In Christ, everything is made right again. He saves us from our sins.

Surely there is more to corporate guilt than just original sin?

Yes, there is. More and more in our time the Church has been speaking about moral issues imbedded in a whole society, like contraception, abortion, pornography, racism, economic injustice, the arms race, and war. These have raised a lot of controversy. It seems that many people can be found to dispute the Church's teaching on any one of them. They express particular annoyance when it seems to them that the issues have little to do with personal morality and the Ten Commandments. Yet, the Catholic bishops rightly struggle to give moral direction on issues of the economy and of international peace and justice because they see that all the people bear responsibility for the whole world. They stand on the principle of solidarity, as the international Synod of Bishops expressed it in Rome in 1971: "Since men are members of the same human family, they are indissolubly linked with one another in the one destiny of the whole world, in the responsibility for which they all share." They recognize, as the Second Vatican Council did, that as the world is strung more closely together by road, airline, and electronic signal, our impact and responsibility reach out to an ever widening circle.

Responsibility for good and evil in the *structures* of society is a hard thing for many people to grasp. This parable of Arthur Simon, founder of Bread for the World, may shed some light on the morality of structures in society and the controversy raised by talking about this morality.

> Once there was a farming town that could be reached by a narrow road with a bad curve in it. There were frequent accidents on the road, especially at the curve, and the preacher would preach to the people of the town to make sure they were Good Samaritans. And so they were, as they would pick the people up on the road, for this was a religious work. One day someone suggested they buy an ambulance to get the accident victims to the town hospital more quickly. The preacher preached and the people gave, for this was a religious work. Then one day a councilman suggested that the town authorize building a wider road and taking out the dangerous curve. Now it happened that the mayor had a farm market right at the curve on the road and he was quite against taking out the curve. Someone asked the preacher to say a word to the mayor and the congregation next Sunday about it. But the preacher and most of the people figured they had better stay out of politics; so next Sunday the preacher preached on the Good Samaritan gospel and encouraged the people to continue their fine work of picking up the accident victims.

As long as that road twisted dangerously, people would be maimed. As long as society clings to dangerous structures, people will be caught in a *situation of sin,* and find it difficult to be good and decent and honest. "What can anyone do?" we tend to say. Well, someone, a lot of someones, have to get around to changing the situation. As a motto put it some years ago: "If you're not part of the solution, you're part of the problem."

And the problem touches more than issues of justice and peace. Ask Father Bruce Ritter of Covenant House about the link between the degradation of children in prostitution and pornography, and the lewd magazines, movies, and plays that apparently decent people purchase and support. "Harmless," they say. "A private matter." But Father Ritter's outraged vision sees their money feeding the evil ring of mobsters, pimps, and pitchmen who have a slice of the pornographic economy. The same can be said about even the casual drug user: He or she contributes to a situation of sin.

Still, in speaking of corporate sin, the last word must be saved for the Bible's basic teaching on morality, that each one must take responsibility for the good and evil in his or her own heart. The source of moral evil in society remains the human heart. This story that a contemplative nun (Marie Beha, O.S.C.) tells on herself illustrates this point and lights up the link between good and evil in any human heart and the situation of good or evil in a wider world:

> A note on the convent dinner table asked for prayers. A public figure had been assassinated. Another one. Who did it? Why? Sister fretted over the questions. She felt the yearning for revenge against the faceless killers. She prayed, of course, as people had asked and as she was bound to do. But who had done it? Then, aware of the confusion and

bitterness of her own heart, she came to this startling answer: "Not 'them, out there.' No, *I* had done it. *I* was involved, deeply so. *I* was guilty." She stayed a long time in the dark chapel, laying her heart and that evil day before her Savior and the Savior of the world.

Well, what has original sin to do with my own life and responsibility?

If we really do believe Jesus is our Savior, it might be well to recall his words: "I have come to call, not the self-righteous, but sinners" (Matthew 9:13). "Of course, we're sinners. Isn't everybody?" we say. That satisfies everything — and nothing. But suppose we sharpen Christ's words to say "I have come to call people who know the evil in them." People of the world have a way of making sin a badge of good fellowship: "Of course, we are all sinners." But they refuse to take responsibility for evil, though not one of them would deny its presence everywhere. Sin and moral evil are the same thing. So, when Christ said "I have come to call sinners," he meant it.

Alexander Solzhenitsyn, Russian exile and great novelist, has come to embody in many minds the role of a prophet: one who tells it as God sees it. Not surprisingly, he has managed to outrage his Communist countrymen and also the United States, his land of refuge. The reason is the same in both places. He has accused both societies of willfully forgetting the difference between good and evil, and of building societies not founded on the most basic human reality, which is morality. Out of his Christian faith he has this to say to every one of us:

> If only there were evil people insidiously committing evil deeds, and it were necessary only to separate them from the rest of us and destroy them. But the line dividing good and evil cuts through the heart of every human being.

But Saint Paul matters far more than Alexander Solzhenitsyn, and he takes great pains with the whole first part of his Letter to the Romans to make the same point: Let everyone look for sin and evil right within himself. He quotes Psalm 14 to say,

> "There is no just man, not even one. . . .
> All have taken the wrong course,
>   all alike have become worthless."
> (Romans 3:10,12)

Pretty grim stuff! And yet, Saint Paul's loving heart yearns to have all of his hearers put themselves in the way of Christ's wonderful words, "I have come to call sinners." If we cannot see the line that divides good and evil within our own hearts, we cannot call on Jesus to be our Savior. Those who wince to see it in the reality of their evil deeds and attitudes know they, too, have been touched by original sin. They make up a hopeful fellowship of sinful people. That would be a pretty good definition of the Catholic Church.

Is it good or bad to feel guilty?

That depends. What has been said thus far offers some common sense in this area. But there are other levels to consider.

On the level of outlook on life — whether from a religious angle or not — people hold some very different opinions. A powerful element of our society denies that the traditional experience of guilt is of much worth at all. For people of this viewpoint there is no God; or if there is one, he lives so far away that he is not bothered by what we do wrong and does not care. Though the Ten Commandments might be useful in forming good citizens and decent neighbors, they are not — in their opinion — the revealed Word of God. They are not binding. Right and wrong are what we choose them to be. If one person sees abortion as good and necessary, so be it. It does not matter that another may hold the opposite conviction. In this view the individual grandly surveys and decrees right and wrong — like a Supreme Being in the moral order. So the paramount issue is choice. Surely we are all aware of the two sides in the abortion issue: pro-life and pro-choice. But the underpinnings of the pro-choice view amount to a rooting out of what we have long called the Judaeo-Christian tradition.

This is our tradition: We believe in a personal, caring God who loves goodness and abhors evil. We believe he has revealed to us a way of life that is very basically expressed in the Ten Commandments. We believe that when we break one of these commandments we naturally feel guilty, for guilty we are.

True, denial of the Commandments gains a kind of freedom. But such freedom involves a lonely trek through a life without God and his guiding hand. We cannot have it both ways. The experience of guilt, though it is unpleasant, is a signal that Someone sees, Someone is there. Cardinal Newman thought that conscience was a proof of the existence of God. To the conscience, guilt feels like shame, which we feel only in the presence of a person. When we shower or bathe we feel no shame in our nakedness. But let us even hear the doorbell ring and we begin to feel hot and nervous. Not even our most secret deliberate thoughts and desires are ours alone. We feel guilty about them if they are evil. Someone is there. Saint Augustine said of him that this Someone is closer to us than we are to ourselves. Maybe these thoughts can give us a better appreciation of Christ's dictum that his yoke is easy and his burden is light. The loss of the Ten Commandments and Christ's teaching would be a desolate freedom indeed.

Some words on the level of public life can be added to those on the level of common sense and outlook on life. Many public figures — politicians, journalists, actors, and others — give a lot of what must be called plain bad example. It seems to have become a matter of principle to some of them to never, never admit the reality of any wrongdoing, even the most outrageous. They deny that the hand in the cookie jar is doing anything wrong.

The example of these people deserves no more respect than their word. That our society — and we as part of it — still pay them money and bestow on them fame or notoriety is nothing new. Hundreds of years ago Erasmus proposed the ironic thesis that base fools succeed best in this world. It is still the same world.

It is a good thing, a gift, to feel guilty when we are so. We hear more and more of tragic people called psychopaths or sociopaths. They feel no remorse for wrongdoing — theft, seduction, murder. They are unable to feel it. They can mimic what other people do when they feel sorry or feel guilty. But they do not experience it themselves. They are not necessarily criminals. They are often charming and they tell good stories. When they marry, their spouses find out there is no feeling beneath the charm and no truth in the stories. They are terribly disfigured persons.

It is something else, however, when people feel guilty even though they are not responsible for what happened. For example, when a priest in the confessional hears someone mention missing Mass on Sunday, he will likely ask whether it was the person's fault. The answer might be, "Well, you see, Father, I was in a skiing accident and I had two broken legs and I was in traction and I was in the hospital. But I feel better telling you!" Actually, there is no problem here; the person really knows there is no guilt.

But what about the following case? A young woman is driving down a quiet city street. She drives carefully enough, well within the speed limit. Two small boys are playing tag on the sidewalk, shielded from her view by a line of parked cars. One of the boys darts into the street and is struck by the young woman's car and is killed. A neighbor who saw the scene from a window runs into the street only to find that the child is already dead. He tells the driver, "Look, I saw the whole thing. It wasn't your fault. You couldn't have seen that kid, and even if you could have seen him, you'd never been able to stop." An investigating policeman tells her the same thing, that she was not to blame. But the young woman cannot bring herself to look into the eyes of the little boy's father as she gasps, "I'm sorry." She does not sleep that night nor the following one. She may become another of those innocent people who lose their minds over unrealistic or even neurotic guilt.

What are some examples of unrealistic guilt?

Unrealistic guilt is a common problem. It shows up in the questions of anguished older parents, "Where did we go wrong, my wife and I? We brought up our children to be

Catholics, even paid for their religious schooling. Now they seem never to go to Church. Where did we go wrong?" These parents may still be grateful that their children live decent lives. But often enough they are ashamed to see them living immorally and recklessly neglecting even to have their children baptized.

There are just too many parents like these to say in general that they have gone wrong. Though it does not resolve their grief, at least they can know they are in the good company of numerous parents like themselves in every Catholic parish. What lays these conscientious people so open to guilt is their knowledge of their own defects of personality and character, which they brought to family life along with their good qualities. Their grown children may even mock these defects and say they are the reasons for their own dismal lives. Yet not even truly negligent parents can be burdened with total responsibility for their children's waywardness. As we said before, it is a premise of our biblical faith that before God we stand individually responsible. There is a severity to this teaching, of course, but that is a small price to pay in exchange for the doom that we might fear is steeped in our genes, or spilled like ink over our birth certificates. We are Christians, not pagans. We refuse to believe that stars and signs determine the events of our lives. We insist that, with the grace of God, we can overcome evil; even that which is deeply and dreadfully living within us. Saint Paul has a motto for us: "It was for liberty that Christ freed us" (Galatians 5:1).

Another example of unrealistic guilt may stem from the death of someone close to us. "If only I had been more kind," one might say. Or another, "If only I had helped more with the housework." Again, "If only we had contacted more doctors." Each "if only" ends with the same statement, that then the deceased would still be alive.

From their eyebrows to the top of their heads these people know that nothing would have made any real difference. But they cannot stop *feeling* that it would. Like anger — even anger at God — such feelings are part of the ordeal of grief, an unbalanced and painful six months or so of mourning. It might be the violence of such a loss that explains the guilt and anger. Here is the survivor still breathing the air and walking the earth, while the one who was so often there with him or her had to be carried off and buried. It just does not seem fair, such a one feels. Someone must be responsible for this. Maybe it is God, or maybe it is the one grieving. Better to blame it on God in angry prayer. He does not mind at all. In his defense, as though he needed one, death was no part of his first plan for us and those we love. Death has entered this world through sin, and for that we must take responsibility.

There are still other examples of unrealistic guilt that may arise from our actions. To place aged parents or an ailing spouse in a nursing home is to know unrealistic guilt. Again, it does not matter that the top of our head knows the correctness of the move. Failure in an important undertaking also carries its burden of guilt feelings. Divorce, being fired from a job, denial of a promotion, failure to gain entrance to a school — all these have us searching for where we went wrong, for what we did wrong, for what we neglected to do. Sometimes the guilt is real and we must then deal with that. Sometimes it is confused or mixed with unrealistic guilt.

By itself, common sense can be a good enough club to beat down unrealistic guilt. We can summon it up ourselves, or a friend can talk some sense into us. The sacrament of Penance affords an opportunity for some plain speaking and at the same time allows for the healing touch of Jesus Christ. "But what if guilt gets out of hand, just goes on and on?" Then we should see a trained psychological counselor, one who can help us out of the swamp of neurotic guilt.

Do other feelings accompany our feelings of guilt?

When people experience guilt they go through a rather complex kind of punishment. Examining the roots of guilt in childhood, psychologists — led by the psychoanalyst Erik Erikson — have noticed first of all that guilt is closely related in childhood to the experience of *shame*. Parents and other people whom we love and *look up to* can sometimes make us feel quite ashamed with just a glance. We want their love and approval, but when they look *that* way or correct us, we feel that we have disappointed them. Erikson says that every experience of shame contains elements of discomfort and agitation. All through life, shame can be mixed in with our experience of guilt, especially if we are people who need the approval of those patterned after our parents.

Sadness or regret also accompany the feeling of guilt. Part of our guilt is the irritation that we have failed ourselves and perhaps offended others. Sometimes this sadness is exaggerated. A friend says, "You should be over that now," but we still feel a deep regret. We cannot forget our faults. At other times it seems that we can casually pass off our responsibility and lazily shrug off any sadness. This can become a problem either to others who are harmed by our lax conscience, or to ourselves when our subconscious quietly upbraids us for not paying attention to our guilt. Psychologists tell us that when we chronically submerge our guilt we often end up punishing ourselves with frequent accidents, ulcers, or depression.

None of these feelings — and indeed guilt itself — are enjoyable. Prophets and psychologists agree that there is only one way to get over guilt — by recognizing it and making up for any real offenses that bother others and nag us.

What reactions accompany the feeling of guilt?

There are many; but here are four prominent ones:

Fear of punishment: The guilty person worries that authorities, whether they may be policemen, parents, or God, will "pay them back" for their failures or offenses.

Inferiority: Dr. Paul Johnson, a minister and psychologist, writes, "Guilt wounds self-respect and confidence by deep feelings of condemnation, remorse and unworthiness." Where we cannot accept God's forgiveness for our past errors, where our guilt goes far beyond our real responsibility, where we tend to blame ourselves even when we are not really guilty, we develop a deep sense of personal inferiority. Self-confidence, on the other hand, grows as we accept forgiveness from God and others, and allow ourselves to rebound from past mistakes.

Anger: Frustration at our past failures leads to anger. We get angry with ourselves and angry at the expectations and demands of others. We become irritated and jealous at the success of others and we cannot forget our past failures. We cannot allow ourselves the realistic calm that comes from admitting that we cannot change the past.

Compulsions: Psychologists note that one mixed-up way of reacting to guilt is the development of compulsions. We *have to* apologize over and over, even when people assure us of forgiveness many times. We *have to* tell the same sins in confession over and over. We *have to* clean and scrub ourselves or our homes, even though anyone can see the shine of cleanliness already. Or, we develop compulsive habits so that we will never make the same mistake again. We *have to* avoid a certain chair, a certain topic of conversation, a certain route to work. Here, guilt is so powerful that we are compelled to develop many rituals to atone for the past and ward off future failings.

How do people adjust to guilt?

There are three ways of adjusting; but only one of them is the right way.

Denial: This is a mental mechanism that allows us to pay no attention to bad things we have done. We "forget" them. After we reveal secret information about a co-worker and have his promotion cancelled, we continue to act with cordiality toward him and pretend to ourselves that we did nothing.

Over-reaction: Sometimes we dwell too much on our possible responsibility for evil. Maybe our friends tell us to forget it, that we are blaming ourselves too much, but we cannot accept their word. For some reason we continue to blame ourselves. Some people live for years with the cloud of unreasonable guilt hanging over them. They cannot experience the forgiveness of others and they cannot forgive themselves.

Apology and restitution: The best and healthiest way to deal with guilt is to apologize and "make up" to those whom we have offended, or to work to improve qualities in ourselves that have led to personal failure. Guilt often takes away the energy we need to improve. The reassurance we get when others accept our apologies restores this energy and enables us to work toward improvement.

Sometimes when I have long periods of depression, I feel vaguely guilty. Why is this?

Throughout this century, psychologists have capitalized on Freud's insight about the connection between guilt and depression. Depression is an *unreasonably* deep experience of sadness and loss. For example, two brothers may be saddened at the sudden death of their father. After a few weeks, one brother still feels the sadness but is able to resume his normal work and relationships with his wife and friends. The other brother still mopes around somewhat aimlessly. His boss complains that he appears careless in his work and he finds himself feeling vaguely guilty during the many periods of sad daydreaming about his father. As the weeks of this sad mood drag on, a competent diagnostician would say that the second brother is experiencing a clinical depression.

In a depression, we cannot adjust to a loss of some kind — the breakup of a love relationship, the death of a close friend, the loss of a job, or some such event. A crucial part of this depression is the deep but often veiled sense of guilt that depressed persons feel about the situation. In a word, they blame themselves for the loss but often do not realize that these guilty feelings lurk in the subconscious. Perhaps one such person may vaguely feel "If only I had told Dad to see a doctor a week before . . . " or "If only I had taken that extra course the boss advised . . . " or "If only I didn't nag my husband about his drinking. . . . " Usually, when these guilty feelings are recognized and faced, the depressed person can see the excessive exaggeration and can pull out of the mood. Sometimes these feelings are hard to recognize because they are part of a pattern of thoughts and feelings that have existed for years and thus make people prone to depression.

Depression-oriented persons take losses harder than average persons. There are two reasons for this. First, they are too self-centered. They exaggerate their own personal importance because they cannot separate their own influence on events and other people from all the other influences upon the same events. They too easily think they could make the difference; they put too much responsibility on themselves. The depressed brother cited above probably could *not* have prevented his father's sudden death, but he worries that he could have. He feels worse than others might because he exaggerates his own importance. Second, depression-prone individuals complicate their self-importance with bad self-concepts of themselves. They have bad opinions of themselves. They easily recall past failures, have a lot of mistaken guilt for past events, and generally are pessimistic about their efforts. This combination of self-importance and bad self-image provides a perfect formula for chronic depression. When losses occur, depressed persons naturally exaggerate their responsibility for the loss and are sure that their failures caused the trouble. They cannot forget easily and go on. They become entangled with moods of guilt, sadness, and self-punishment.

Modern medicine has found that chemical imbalances in the brain and nervous system help to make people prone to depression. With medication, people are able to pull out of these moods much more quickly because self-forgetting activity, especially somewhat strenuous activity, helps to change these moods. Medication promotes activity, enables the person to put self-centered worries out of mind, and soon the mood disappears.

Along with medication, long-term spiritual direction or therapy can also help depression-prone persons to get to the roots of their bad self-concept, overcome some of the self-directed anger, and anticipate — as well as prevent — exaggerated guilt reactions.

Years ago I was a heavy drinker. Once when I was drunk I ran over a young boy who died as a result of the accident. The months in jail and years of probation sobered me up. Now, fifteen years later I still feel guilty.

The moral law and the civil laws of most states recognize our guilt for actions that we should have foreseen. When we drink and drive we become as dangerous to others as armed criminals. The moral law insists that mature people should look ahead and realize the harm that can come from their negligence.

Sometimes people try to banish their guilt by saying, "I didn't want to hurt the kid," or "I only wanted to relax a little. I didn't realize I wouldn't be able to control the car." These rationalizations cannot absolve us of our responsibility or guilt. We are obliged to think of the consequences of our actions.

Still, as the Redemptorist theologian, Father Bernard Häring, in *The Law of Christ,* stresses: "The guilt, however, and it is important not to overlook this point, is not so serious as the guilt of the premeditated offense." God understood the complexities of this man's drinking and his lack of responsibility. By confessing his sorrow to God and paying the price for his crime, he has atoned for his negligence. Still, even though God has forgiven him and wiped the slate clean, like all of us he does not find it easy to forget these tragic events of the past. The sadness and guilt linger for the rest of his life. He can, however, see the merciful hand of God in this tragedy. First, for his own reasons,

God chose that time to call that innocent youngster to himself. Second, with the help of his grace, this man has turned this tragedy into a chance to change his life and get closer to God. Even though the memory of the accident will not go away, he can use it as an opportunity to thank God for waking him up and helping him to put aside a dangerous way of life.

I keep worrying about the decisions and the choices I make. How do I know I did the right thing or am doing the right thing?

That is a difficult question to answer. To deal with it in its strict sense would require two things that no human being can muster: knowledge of the future and control over its direction. If by "the right thing" we mean that which is correct, effective, and salutary by common opinion, we are chasing a mirage. Even if at one time a decision may seem to have been a good one, a year or two later it may look altogether different. Not too long ago everyone seemed to be saying that Harry Truman was a poor president. Within the last few years he has begun to look very good. What changed? Certainly not his decisions.

By looking back at some decisions we might have taken — ones that turned out well for us — we might catch a deeper truth about what is correct or right. Maybe some years ago we purchased a piece of property that turned out to be a profitable investment. People may be saying we made a shrewd decision. But we know that because of a zoning ordinance change a large corporation settled its headquarters nearby and this increased the value of our property. It was just luck on our part. Only God can see and control the future. Yet, even he holds his Last

Judgment only when all human decisions or omissions have fully run their course.

To demand "the right thing" of ourselves is unreasonable. But to accept the responsibility of making the best decision we can and then living with it as it plays itself out — this is required of anyone who would claim to be a mature man or woman. On the other hand, to put off a decision — whether to marry, to go to college, to join the Army — until we are sure it is the right thing, can well be a disguise for a lack of basic faith and nerve. There is no excuse for not taking counsel and then praying to make the best decision as one sees it — the *best* one, not necessarily the *right* one. One aid to this is the truth that God is our judge. He sees the heart, not just "the bottom line," as our society cruelly calls it. God is not like the baseball owners who fired the manager after a losing season even though no one could have done better with the same team. God is a far easier judge than this world is, which seems to write down all losers for fools.

How does the sacrament of Penance work on our guilt?

The action of the sacrament of Penance combines two very important and healthy ingredients: our activity in preparing for and confessing our sins, and God's activity of embracing us in forgiveness through the sacramental activity of the Church. Both are important for dealing with our guilt.

As we prepare to confess our sins, we naturally examine our lives and consciences. We look to the past, measure our actions against the norms of the commandments and beatitudes, and see where we have done badly. Sometimes our shame and guilt is very clear to us. At other times we are somewhat casual about our dishonesty, adultery, or uncharitableness; and this is because our emotions can trick us. Nevertheless, we try to probe our consciences to enter the sacramental room and apologize to God and seek his pardon. It is important that during our self-examination we sort out our feelings of guilt. Maybe in some cases in which we have developed a calloused conscience we should let more guilt seep into our awareness. We should *feel* bad about selfishly cheating a fellow worker out of a promotion or neglecting our supervision of our teenagers. So often we catch the diseases of our society — coolness in our responsibilities toward others, forgetfulness about the harm our selfishness brings to others. Then this thorough self-examination can help us to know what to say to God, what bruises to show to his healing touch. Confession works on our guilt, first of all, by helping us to notice where we feel guilty and more importantly, where we *should* feel guilty.

Then, as we confess our sins and talk about our guilt, God's activity begins. The priest whispers words of encouragement, admonition, and hope. The words of absolution remind us that "God, the Father of mercies . . . " wishes to reconcile us to himself and through the death of his Son and the activity of his Spirit, holds out pardon and peace to us. What a relief! Throughout the centuries many people have felt their guilt disintegrate with the Church's absolution. Millions of men and women have felt a closeness to God and the healing touch of his mercy. Guilt that has been overwhelming has melted like ice in a summer sun.

Both aspects are crucial to God's healing of our guilt. We need to "be in touch with" our guilt, to honestly look at our past, and to apologize through our confession. Then our faith and sorrow let us experience God's forgiveness as we unload the baggage of our guilt.

Why do I keep thinking of my past sins?

This question reveals a very common problem. Sins already repented of and confessed come repeatedly to mind, along with the worry that somehow they are not over and done with, not forgiven. We speak of our past catching up with us or coming back to haunt us. Some people read this anxiety as a sign that God still holds the past against them.

Something good can result from this problem, however. Nearly always the people who ask this question are better and deeper people than they were when they committed the sins that now trouble them. All too often a priest will hear the confession of a grave sin — let's say of an abortion. And often enough, he will hear the penitent say, "Father, at the time it didn't seem like any big deal. But now I see, now I see." At the time of the sin that person may have been so ignorant, so confused and frightened, that the terrible deed was not a grave sin in the eyes of God and in the estimation of conscience.

This brings up an important point: *We are guilty of our sins as we saw them at the time of their commission, not as we see them at the present moment.* We do not acquire the mark of a grave sin because now we see, as then we did not. The damage may be just as real, as in an abortion, but the guilt really weighing on the conscience may not even require that we confess it. For only clearly grave and deliberate sin must be confessed. Still, confession will greatly assist in dealing with a delayed feeling of guilt.

But what is happening when the past comes as a frequent intruder into our quiet moments? Is God tracking us down, as war criminals are relentlessly tracked down over many years so that they may be punished? No, it is not God. It is our human nature, wounded and twisted by our sins, that cries out for redress. Saint Thomas Aquinas says that God is merciful, but nature is not. We have been taught that if ever we commit a grave sin, we should immediately address a prayer of love and sorrow to him, and he would forgive us at once. Such is the power of what is called an act of perfect contrition. Such is the mercy of God. (We still have to submit our sin to the priest in confession, however.) We also remember that something remained to be dealt with even then. Though no longer periled by eternal damnation, we still face what is called the temporal punishment due to sin. This is the consequence, this side of eternity, for what we have done wrong. It is nature's pound of flesh.

Awareness of the ecology, which has gained our serious attention, may help us understand this better. We have gotten used to the idea that we must be very careful of what we spew into the sky, because it will fall down on us again, perhaps to poison our water or foul our lungs. The earth we walk on is also unforgiving. We have grown very frightened of what we might be drinking in our water because we have been careless of what we have buried in the ground. The same rules also apply to human life. We are always telling ourselves that we should be more careful of what and how much we eat, of how much we exercise. These rules also apply morally, even in mixed cases like smoking or drinking too much. Mark Twain is supposed to have joked: "It's easy to give up smoking. I've done it hundreds of times." But smoking is no joking matter anymore. Or consider the married couple who have suffered an infidelity, maybe a mutual infidelity. Let us say that by the grace of God and their own good will they have reconciled and taken up a peaceable life again. But how difficult it will be when one of them is away on a trip for the other not to suspect again. And in a heated argument it will not be easy to refrain from harping back to a former infidelity. Such in part are the temporal punishments due to sin.

There is a link here with the doctrine of Purgatory, that state of purification that deals with the harm of sin to our human nature and person. The whole idea is that before we enter into eternal life with God, all the old injuries must be healed, all the misshapen bones reset, all the mangled limbs resewn and stirred to graceful form and use. This holds more in a moral and spiritual sense, of course, rather than a strictly physical one. And this is what is meant by the work of penance and amendment of life that we promise to undertake when we go to confession. It is a work of *repair*. Only God, of course, has the skill and power to erase and undo evil and rebuild our lives and persons. But we do work along with him. We are like stroke victims cooperating with a masterful physical therapist who enables us to walk and talk once again.

Here is a particular example that will help us see a little more into this wondrous mystery of God's forgiveness. A rather old gentleman is a favorite of his neighborhood. One day a young man is telling an older neighbor how much he admires that old man. With no malice at all, the neighbor says, "Yes, he really is a delight. But you should have known him years ago. He was a horror to man, God, and beast." And so he was. But he had time. And he probably also had a patient wife and family. He was remade, repaired. But if he had not been given the time, there would still be Purgatory. Though it is a place of pain, it is not the dreadful state of hell where the pain is caused by hatred. Purgatory's pain is caused by our lack of love for God and for all

God's creatures whom we may have injured during our earthly lives.

The prescription, then, for dealing with guilt over past repented sins is to join God in the work of repair. The same people who are troubled by this anxiety very often also say that they are trying to "make up for" the past. This is another expression for repair or reparation. If they have committed an abortion, they might contribute to or work for agencies that aid pregnant women to have their babies. If they have willfully neglected their own parents, now deceased, they might visit nursing homes and sponsor some entertainments for the residents. Prayerfully they offer these small efforts to God, knowing that they are like children who help their fathers rebuild a house by struggling to hand him just one brick. In fact, as time goes on, they might give themselves above all to prayer, for their own sake and for the sake of a whole world that needs to be forgiven and repaired.

When I was a teenager I engaged in some shameful sexual acts. I told them in confession just before my marriage and several other times, but my guilt won't go away.

We believe that when we make a sincere confession, God mercifully forgives us. Usually we feel relief after we have confessed things for which we feel a lot of shame. Two human difficulties, however, often arise. First, as time goes on our faith becomes weaker and we begin to wonder whether God really "forgives and forgets." We should be assured that he does. Just as he lovingly gave complete forgiveness to Mary Magdalene, Peter, and the thief on the cross, he forgives us, no matter what we have done. When these doubts come to mind, we should pray for a deeper faith because the devil is trying to take away the peace that we should experience with God's forgiveness. As our faith grows stronger, our trust in God's mercy will deepen, and we will know that our sincere confession brought God's total pardon of our sins.

The other difficulty, as psychologists point out, comes not from a failure on the part of God's forgiveness but from the fact that so many of us cannot forgive ourselves. Maybe as children we built up exaggerated demands on ourselves. We had to be *perfect*. And if we failed, we thought we could never live it down. Other people can accept our apologies, a priest can say we are forgiven, but we cannot forgive ourselves! How sad! Our extra-strict superego robs us of God's peace. Although he offers us release, we continue to imprison ourselves within our own twisted guilt. God wants us to know he has forgiven us, but we won't pay attention. We lack his patience with ourselves. We demand more from ourselves than God himself does. Unless we are certain that we will never stray from perfection, we cannot relax. Most of all, we cannot pull up that anchor of shame mired in the past and sail forward with God's love. Sometimes, with the help of a regular confessor or spiritual director, we can overcome this overdemanding conscience. We should realize, however, that this is basically an emotional and not strictly a religious problem. Sometimes we may need psychiatric help if past guilt and shame persist for years. The goal of the medicine or the therapy would be to remove those psychological obstacles to our experience of God's mercy and pardon.

For the past year my best friend has felt terribly guilty about the breakup of her seventeen-year marriage. She feels

that she was somehow at fault, even though her husband left her for another woman. She feels very guilty and this is beginning to affect her children. What can I do?

Right now this woman is one of the best resources that her divorced friend has. Physically, she cannot do very much; but she can support her friend in many important ways.

To help the most she has to start with the awareness that she cannot do everything. She cannot bring back her friend's husband. She cannot raise her children for her. She cannot climb inside her heart and turn off the faucets of worry and guilt. Because of her friend's confusion, she has to realize that her friend will probably not take (or even hear) most of her good advice. Understanding these limitations, she then can begin to help her friend resolve her guilt and put her life back together.

The place to begin is the willingness she has to spend time with her friend and listen to her. She should encourage her to talk about her guilt. No doubt, in view of her husband's infidelity and his abandonment of his family, her friend's evil deeds will be comparatively small. But this wife will no doubt wonder if she should have noticed changes in him earlier, if she could have changed qualities in herself that may have irritated him. This friend should let her talk about these worries, about her anger and her sense of loss. She should not tell her friend not to "feel bad." Her friend will feel bad, despite any insistent advice. But, as she talks and re-examines her part in the matter, she will gradually see things more realistically. She will still have many regrets — her dreams have been shattered — but gradually the debilitating guilt will be lessened.

Next, it will be important for this divorced woman to get involved with others and to engage in activities of her own. A helpful program to get over loss and guilt involves physical activity and groups of friends. She should not be allowed to mope around. She should be encouraged to do things with her children and to be as busy and active as she can.

Finally, this good friend can help the divorced woman to experience the healing that God offers to people who have to suffer. "Come to me, all you who are weary and find life burdensome, and I will give you rest" is Christ's promise. He can give peace and consolation and energy far beyond the talents of the best human friend. He understands this woman's loss, her anger, and her guilt. One who would really be a friend to her should encourage her, pray with her, get her to stop by and pray alone in church or attend an occasional daily Mass. The Lord will respond to her needs and her tears. Maybe a priest can be found for some spiritual direction. Most of all, a good friend can assure her that God does not want her to carry this cross alone, that he will soothe her guilt and give her strength for the future.

Last year my fifteen-year-old daughter got pregnant. I insisted on and paid for an abortion. My husband is bitter. He claims I should feel guilty for killing the unborn baby. But I did not will the killing. I just wanted my daughter freed from a tragic pregnancy that would have ruined her future.

Sad to say, this woman's husband is right. She is guilty of using coercion on her daughter and of killing the unborn child. The Gospels stress that the end does not justify the means. We cannot shield ourselves from the shadow of guilt by claiming that we did not want the direct result of our action. This woman's insistence led to the death of the unborn child and until she faces her responsibility, she will not be able to ask God's pardon and shake the effects of her sinful action.

Moreover, she probably overestimated the damage which the pregnancy would cause her daughter. Many young women make mistakes, but these mistakes often push them to greater maturity and even to deeper closeness with God. Perhaps some childless couple could have adopted and loved that daughter's child. Finally, there is a good possibility that the daughter will carry deep and exaggerated guilt into the future for something that her mother basically forced on her. This mother should pray that her daughter will experience God's healing. We have to say that sometimes momma does *not* know best.

So much of this sounds so grim and negative — guilt, shame, evil. Isn't the whole point of life to do good? Why not stress that?

Good point, though it is perhaps overstated. The most basic dictum of morality has both a positive and negative side: Good must be done; evil must be avoided. Why, then, do we emphasize the negative so much? Probably because of the burden of guilt upon our human nature. Suppose a large group of people were asked to mention the first thought or word that comes to their mind after hearing the word "conscience." Probably most of them would say "guilty." How many would say that "good," or "upright," or "peaceful" came as their first thought? Not too many.

The writers of the New Testament reflect this common

human experience. They understand the word and idea of conscience in the same way that contemporary Greek-speaking people understand it. For those people conscience is almost always *guilty* conscience. And this is why Saint Paul does not make conscience, even a peaceful conscience, the be-all and end-all of religion. He implies this in one of his Letters when he says that although his conscience is clear, that sense does not justify him (see 1 Corinthians 4:4-5). In general, conscience comes into play when we step over some forbidden moral line, over the edge, so to speak. The safest way of dealing with this edge would be to sit down or stand still. Yet, Saint Paul knows that Christian life can never stand still, that it can never say "finished" to the job of loving God and loving God's people. He knows our Lord's parable of the talents or the silver pieces, and the condemnation of the man who thought he would safely bury the money and dig it up to return it to his master (see Matthew 25:14-30). He knows the Sermon on the Mount. Who could ever accomplish that project of goodness and moral beauty in a hundred lifetimes?

So, especially as our moral and religious life deepens and strengthens, our conscience shows us another and brighter face. It becomes, as theologian Romano Guardini described it, the organ of God and his work of accomplishing all good in all the world and all time. It helps us to see and prompts us to do the good things we can do for our own small worlds and the people in them, even if these are only "my good deeds for the day."

This work of doing good is not so clearly laid out as the concrete evils we must avoid are enumerated in the Ten Commandments. Therefore, we must pray to see what good the Lord God wants us to do. "Thy kingdom come, thy will be done." These phrases of the Our Father say it for us. If we truly ask to see, we will see.

(The next question involves this striving to figure what good can be done in a real situation.)

I am a health teacher in our county junior high school. Once a week I teach a sex education program to eighth graders. I feel a little guilty and worried. The text clearly describes different kinds of sexual activity and gives very vague moral guidelines to the boys and girls.

This teacher finds herself in a difficult moral position. On the one hand, as a public school teacher, she cannot bring specifically religious teachings into her work with the teenagers. On the other hand, she is correct in seeing how much guidance young people need to deal with the exploitation of sex in our culture and with their own growing interest in sexual activity.

Although educational officials may be content if she merely presents the material in the textbook, she does have a God-given responsibility to give some moral guidance to teenagers. Often, even their parents feel awkward about offering this moral guidance. Also, teenagers can give the impression of being sophisticated and knowledgeable about sex when they really are confused and do not want to seem naïve to their friends.

Actually, even without quoting from the Bible or from Church teaching, she can do quite a bit. Even people without religious interests see the danger of precocious sexual activity on the part of teenagers. Dr. Sol Gordon at the 1982 annual meeting of the American Association of Sex Educators, Counselors, and Therapists had this to say about present teenage sexual activity: "What is going on is a national social disaster."

In addition to information, as a health and sex education teacher she can offer important guidance to teenagers. These boys and girls are at a most vulnerable time in their lives. She can spot kids who face special difficulties because of divorce in the family, of moving to a new school or neighborhood, or of rejection by other teens. Although curiosity and stimulation are widespread among American teens, it is often *loneliness* or fear of rejection that pushes teenagers into sexual activity. This teacher's notice of troubled teens, her encouragement of wholesome friendships, and her willingness to spend some time listening to worried teenagers can do much to offset the temptations of our culture and the neglect of parents. Finally, perhaps she could encourage her parish church to provide programs for young people, and offer her services to programs already in place. She has a lot of experience to share.

Many people look back with appreciation and thanks to coaches, teachers, and other adults who helped them get through serious difficulties as teenagers. This teacher's worry and sense of guilt can lead to real help for the teenagers she teaches. It will not be easy to walk the tightrope of offering prudent information and guidance beyond the textbook, but she seems to have the will and the means to find ways to really help her students.

Conclusion

We conclude these questions and answers about wrong conduct by calling to mind the element of *fact* in guilt, especially when the evil we have actually done still damages our lives and the lives of others. The abortion that, at the time seemed to be "no big deal," still quenched a human life, a loss that cannot be restored. Another child may be born, but not *that* one. What if we really did lack respect for our parents who are now gone and cannot hear us say we are sorry? What if we did indeed badly bring up our wayward children, did indeed wreck a marriage that could have endured with a little more work and prayer? And outside of our own personal lives, what of the horrors we see on the TV and in the papers, the massacres, murders, extortions, meaningless wars? Maybe we deal with them by turning the page or changing the channel or by switching our attention to the next tragedy. But they remain. Who deals with all that evil?

Jesus does. He is Savior; his name means Savior. He carries off what we cannot bear even to think about. He saves us from our sins. He came to forgive sin. "Jesus saves." Perhaps those two words are pasted and splashed on more fences, walls, and billboards than any other slogan in our land. We may even think all that exposure wears out their meaning. But it does not. We need someone to save us from the crushing burden of guilt.

They say that when rajahs still lived in India, and one of them was dying, he would call to his bedside a holy man. The dying rajah would lay on the holy man all the sins of his life. He would also give the holy man one thousand rupees. With the rajah's sins and the thousand rupees, he would leave the country, never to return. Strange, is it not? Yet, we know what the rajah was trying to do. He was having the holy man carry off his guilt like dangerous waste to a desolate place. In the Old Testament the high priest would pray the sins of the people onto the scapegoat, while he imposed his hands on the goat's head. Then he would drive it out to the desert, to perish along with all the sins (see Leviticus 16). Again, we know what those people were seeking.

We do not have a goat; we have a Lamb. We do not have a holy man; we have the Son of God. "Lamb of God, you take away the sins of the world." We say that at every Mass. We say it, even sing it, three times. Like a sanitation engineer, he carries off what would fill our homes, block our driveways, stop our streets. It is not that we are too heedless to get down to cleaning things up. We cannot bear evil's weight, or touch it; for it would crush and poison us. But for our sake and in our place, Jesus Christ took on the lashes, mockings, spital, blows, and wounds that were all our sins. He dragged them down to death with him, as into a deep black lake. After three days he broke through the surface, alive again. The sins remained at the bottom, in hell.

Why did he do such a thing? Because he loves us. That explains everything and nothing, because love is such a mystery. Even merely human love is such a mystery. Some people cannot accept love, believing that they must earn or deserve it. So it is with the young man who cannot bear to marry the young woman who loves him — and whom he loves — because past escapades make him feel sordid and unworthy. Another young man may have the same past and yet have the memory of it enlarge his joy that he still has the love of so good a woman. He knows he does not deserve it. But he sees that merit is here beside the point. All real love is freely given; it cannot be bought or earned. Above all, this is true of God's love, which we call *grace*. It is gratis, free. Free, yes, but never cheap. It dearly costs both lover and beloved. All the years of a married life are a measure of what it costs.

So, the cost of Christ's love for us is his Passion, death, and Resurrection. Yet he freely paid it, even yearned to pay it, as he saw his death ahead of him. That is something we cannot question because it has no explanation. But then neither does anyone's falling in love have any explanation. We sometimes reject Christ's dearly won grace because we cannot understand it, because we know we do not deserve it, because — as sometimes we say it out loud — we cannot forgive ourselves. If by forgiving ourselves we mean successfully laboring to cancel past evils, well, we are then exactly right. Hopelessly right. Even very good and holy people make the mistake of traveling back to some terrible past sin or time of sin and wondering whether and how it is forgiven. Two terrible results come of such a mistake. First — especially in matters like lust, anger, and resentment — the past sin takes life again in the form of a serious temptation to commit the same sin. Second, and worse, the memory of the past sin causes discouragement and doubt of God's forgiveness. Such a going back is surely a ploy of the one called Satan, who constantly accuses all of us. "See what you did," we hear in our conscience, and dwelling on it, soon find our confidence failing us. We do well to be careful of "bad thoughts," usually sexual thoughts. We do even better to be careful of these accusatory thoughts, which can lead us to abandon all hope.

Jesus Christ, the Lamb of God, died for us. He is our Savior. Nothing more can be said, and nothing more can be explained. We can do no more than gaze on him in the Host at Mass and pray for his mercy and his peace, and then reach out needily to consume him. All we can do is gaze on a Crucifix and see the truth of the words of Blessed Juliana of Norwich as they apply to our life and our world: "The worst has already happened, but it has been repaired. And all will be well, and all will be well, and all will be very well."

Other helpful books from Liguori

HOW TO FORGIVE YOURSELF AND OTHERS
Steps to Reconciliation
by Rev. Eamon Tobin

Presents a simple, yet effective plan of personal and interpersonal healing that begins with "wanting to really want to forgive." Points out our role in the forgiving and renewal process as well as our dependence upon God's help. **$1.50**

THE SACRAMENT OF PENANCE
Its Past and Its Meaning for Today
by Rev. Eamon Tobin

Traces the historical unfolding of the sacrament showing how it has been updated — not outdated — and suggests how you can best use it to find growth and peace. Includes a contemporary Examination of Conscience. **$1.50**

HELPS FOR THE SCRUPULOUS
by Russell M. Abata, C.SS.R., S.T.D.

Some people are haunted by worry almost beyond human endurance. No amount of reassurance seems to set them at ease. This offers some guidelines for relief. A first-aid kit for the scrupulous and a handy guide for counselors. **$2.95**

Order from your local bookstore or write to:
Liguori Publications, Box 060, Liguori, Missouri 63057
(Please add 75¢ for first item ordered and 25¢ for each additional item for postage and handling.)